DREAMSCAPE
2020

DREAMSCAPE
2020

Erik Rask

ISBN: 979-8-89316-664-4 (Paperback)
ISBN: 979-8-89316-663-7 (Ebook)

Acknowledgements

Special thanks to my editing team:
Mariah, Emma, Qatarina, and Christina
at Wandering Words Media.

Dedication

Humbly dedicated to all those who lost loved ones in 2020, to the ones lost, and to the baby whale pretending, that held my shoulders diving in the crystalline sea on languid, shut-down days, when the world got quiet for a bit; and to the many others who joined or supported me on the long, mad journey leading to this little book—with all my love, appropriate apologies, and deep, deep gratitude.

—E.R.

Contents

"To subdue matter is the first step, to realize the ideal is the second."

—VICTOR HUGO

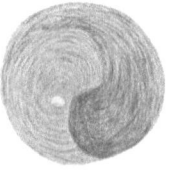

CHAPTER 1

The Pearl

There was an infinite expanse of black space. It was filled with small, white pinpricks of light poking through the blackness. Some of these pinpricks were dim, appearing far away. Some were bright, appearing closer. Behind, the light of billions of such pinpricks, too far off to be discerned individually, joined in a cloudy band of faint light stretching across the black space behind.

Turning, another light appeared. This one was no small pinprick; rather, it was a giant, terrifying ball of fire very close by. It boiled as energy from within reached the surface, trying to escape, but getting pulled by incredible gravity back to the core, to stay for eons before trying again to escape. At intervals, however, some did reach the surface, escaping as geysers shooting out into the surrounding blackness.

After some time, turning still, the terrifying ball of energy was no longer in view. Facing once again the expansive, infinite blackness, the same small pinpricks of white light poked through, just as before. Some were dim, some were bright. Some appeared close, some far off. Behind, the cloudy band of white light still glowed. It was still, peaceful, and serene.

Now, however, there was something else. It was no bigger than the little white pinpricks of light poking through the black, but it was blue.

Turning slowly still, the terrifying ball of energy came into view again, so close and so harsh and so bright in contrast to the blackness and pinpricks in the opposite direction, so far away.

When the blackness and small points of light returned, the blue point of light among the many white pinpricks had grown bigger. It was now much bigger than the little white pinpricks. It shined a brilliant, bright blue. It was getting closer.

The terrifying ball of energy came into view again, washing out the black. It stayed for some time, then the blackness returned. The small pinpricks were there, as before, filling the field of blackness.

This went on, brightness, blackness, terrifying brightness, peaceful and serene blackness with sparkling pinpricks of white—each time, the blue object growing larger and brighter.

At last, it passed close by. It was an oasis, floating in nothingness. On its surface were swirling storm clouds, land masses of red, yellow, and green, white ice at its top and bottom, and a blue, shimmering ocean filling everything in between. Around the circumference of this majestic ball was a halo of blue. It seemed the eye of the heavens, glimpsing its own image in still water, soon to be blown away in the breeze.

Turning and turning, the terrifying ball of energy came into view once again, washing out the black. It stayed for some time, then the blackness returned. Round and round this continued—blackness, intense brightness, blackness, intense brightness— each time the shining blue pearl getting smaller and smaller, before disappearing finally around the Sun.

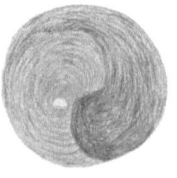

CHAPTER 2

The Moon

His eyes opened, fixing on a thing laying on the ground nearby. It was different from the hard, dry dirt and rocks around it. It looked soft. It had tiny hairs that bent slightly in the breeze. His eyes drifted to the long grass rustling above, and the black sky, then back to the soft-looking thing on the ground.

Then, it moved.

The still picture of before turned to a blur of black and silver. There was a grunting sound, followed by heavy breathing. He was standing now, looking out over a sea of grass that stretched to a far, far away line. There, it met a dome of blackness. He slowly turned his head, wondering at the dome of blackness and small pinpricks of light above.

There were thousands of points of light, some bright and others dim, some flashing—red, blue, red, blue, or blue, green, blue, green. Behind, very faint, was a thick, cloudy band of white light stretching across the sky. Across the zenith of the sky, following the path of cloudy, mysterious light, his eyes rested upon the Moon.

It hung low over the horizon, glowing a blood red over the grass that blew in endless waves. On its face were mountains, canyons, vast plains, ancient lava flows, and pockmarks of meteor impacts with bright debris fields surrounding them. It grew redder and slowly sank, stretching and distorting as it finally disappeared. He stared in wonder after it was gone.

He took a deep breath of the breeze that was blowing on his skin, unconsciously placing his hands on his chest as he did. Inside, he felt a strange, rhythmic beating.

Seeing now that they were his, he held his hands before his eyes. The skin was cracked from dryness, resembling the parched earth of dirt and rocks. There were great networks of tiny lines. Tendons and veins bulged from the backs of the hands. He opened and closed them, moving each finger one by one.

He then looked down at his torso and waist, his legs and the feet he stood upon. He lifted a foot, brushing the stones off that were pressing into it.

Between his legs a strange appendage hung, atop a sack with two balls inside.

He looked outward again. Now, only the stars remained, turning red as they fell one by one over the horizon. The picture above him was moving. The thing he stood on spun.

He lifted a foot again, now placing it in front of the other. He did this again. He felt off-balance at first, but soon steadied. The long grass brushed against his legs. He was moving now, slowly through the grass. His steps soon quickened. His breathing grew heavier. He went west, the direction the Moon had gone.

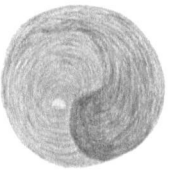

CHAPTER 3

The Jungle

Deep in the jungle, there lived a band of monkeys. Two males routinely shared the role of alpha, fighting between each other for control of the territory and the other monkeys. They were about equal size and strength. Power thus went back and forth, back and forth. Each was supported by one half or the other of the monkeys in the canopy and forest floor below. They had slightly different ideas about life in the jungle, on how food should be shared, how the elderly should be cared for, etc.

But neither were the real Alpha. The real Alpha ruled from the shadows, keeping the two in his employ. The balance between the two kept the monkeys in the jungle at bay and generally satisfied, if not complacent. The two gave the others below a sense of choice.

Things went on like this in the jungle for many years, but dissatisfaction with the leadership of the two alpha pretenders grew. One day, a challenger, sensing the moment, climbed the canopy, expressing the grievances of the many others below:

> "Let us wage a moral and political war
> against the billionaires and corporate
> leaders, on Wall Street and elsewhere,
> whose policies and greed are destroying
> the middle class of America!"[1]

The monkeys on the forest floor ran about wildly, hooting and hollering, whipped into a frenzy at such words. The two alpha pretenders were uneasy, but agreed to assist the other in fending off the challenger with slander and promises of disaster. The monkeys below resorted to what they knew— the rule of the two pretenders.

Then another challenger climbed the canopy, offering a different sort of message:

> "We pledge to you that we will root
> out the communists, Marxists, fascists,
> and the radical left thugs that live like
> vermin within the confines of our

---

[1]   Bernie Sanders (@SenSanders), Twitter, April 28, 2012, 12:35 p.m., https://x.com/SenSanders/status/196729368842739712.

> country… Because if you have a capable,
> competent, smart, tough leader—
> Russia, China, North Korea—they're
> not going to want to play with us."[2]

The monkeys on the forest floor were again excited at such words, running about wildly. Their hooting and hollering again echoed through the jungle as they beat their chests, running about, breaking small trees as they went.

But the anger spilled over into fighting among the monkeys themselves. The long-haired monkeys fought with the short haired. The hunters fought the gatherers. Division grew.

The pretender alphas and the real Alpha smiled as chaos consumed the jungle. But so did the Alpha of a rival band in the same jungle, sensing opportunity.

---

[2] "Trump holds Veterans Day rally in New Hampshire." 2023. YouTube video, 14:30, posted by LiveNOW from FOX, November 11, 2023, https://www.youtube.com/watch?v=c7zvn9rLiSM.

CHAPTER 4

The Scene

As Dawn stretched her rosy arms over the sweeping green spaces of monuments, museums, and grand government buildings of Washington, D.C., a line of tired-looking people stood against a wall outside the Walmart Supercenter on H Street. Gene was also standing there with a suitcase he had bought at the Salvation Army days before.

It was a very cold morning in D.C. Gene had tried to sleep in the airport terminal upon arriving, beneath a giant Stars and Stripes banner in the empty terminal, but it was too cold. Once the train started to run, getting more clothes was top priority.

When the store opened, the tired-looking people slowly shuffled inside. Gene went in too, pulling the suitcase on its wheels. He left the suitcase with the guard in front of the store and went in search of the men's clothing department.

The store was chaos. The aisles were filled with large cardboard boxes and stacks of clothes in wrinkled piles, needing to be folded or hung up. A large black man stood staring at the long johns, and Gene joined him, trying to figure out what size he was. He put several in the basket, along with a black hoodie and beige denim jacket, then headed to the front of the store to pay. He then headed outside, rolling the suitcase from Salvation Army into the streets of D.C.

Heading south, he came to the east portico of the Capitol, where, in 1961, President John F. Kennedy sent out a call for self-sacrifice to the Baby Boomers, the earliest of whom were just coming of age:

> "Ask not what your country can do for you; ask what you can do *for your country!*"

Power emanated from the old building, captured in its architecture. The majestic yet forbidding old building and its high gray dome stood somberly against the pale blue of the morning sky behind it. It was surrounded with hundreds and hundreds of feet of fencing, and plastic yellow tape that said:

> CAUTION—POLICE LINE—
> DO NOT CROSS

A large, yellow security gate made an entrance, where two Capitol guards chatted with one another. One of the guards wore a camouflage hunting hat and had a thick goatee. He looked askance toward Gene, then turned back to bullshitting with the other.

The yellow gate lifted, and the guards let pass a black SUV with very dark tinted windows. It went several hundred feet past the barricade then stopped at the steps of the Capitol. A man and a woman got out, both in black suits. The lady's hair blew around wildly in the breeze. They were too far away to recognize as they disappeared behind steps and into the Capitol.

Gene rolled the suitcase from Salvation Army to the giant marble steps of the United States Supreme Court. From the base of the steps, behind the barricade, he made out the silhouette of a lonesome guard pacing between the massive marble columns supporting the pediment of the highest Court in the land, at the top of which were the words, engraved in stone:

EQUAL JUSTICE UNDER LAW

Gene made his way around the Capitol building and looked across the length of the National Mall. A million marchers had filled the space in 1963, when

Dr. Martin Luther King Jr. delivered a speech from the steps of the Lincoln Memorial, in which he said:

> "Now is the time to make justice a
> reality for all of God's children!"[3]

Today, there was just a lonely vendor truck in the windswept middle, with paraphernalia of bright red, white, and blue hung on display, blowing around in the frigid breeze.

The figure of Abraham Lincoln was barely visible. He sat in his chair at the Lincoln Memorial with his stern look directed eastward toward those walking in the halls of Congress and sitting in their quiet chambers of the Supreme Court. His admonishing eyes reminded all about the solemn oath to protect the promises of Liberty made to Ourselves and our Posterity, enshrined in our U.S. Constitution, which so many have died to keep.

Gene stopped to rip off the outer layer of plastic on the wheels of the suitcase from Salvation Army. They were already falling apart on the rough dirt paths of the National Mall. He finally reached the Washington Monument, pointing up at the sky. He then crossed Constitution Avenue.

---

[3] American Rhetoric, 2024, "I Have a Dream", speech delivered by Dr. Martin Luther King Jr., August 28, 1963, https://www.americanrhetoric.com/speeches/mlki-haveadream.htm.

Behind a high black fence, a maze of street cones, a sea of black and white SUVs, expansive lawns, and large trees which looked tiny in the distance was a speck of pink, gleaming bright in the morning sun. It was the White House, or as the website says:

> ". . . . the *People's* House, where we
> hope *all* Americans feel a sense
> of inclusion and belonging."[4]

He walked up 17th Street, passing large buildings of the Organization of American States, Daughters of the American Revolution National Headquarters, American Red Cross National Headquarters, Federal Reserve Board, Federal Deposit Insurance Corporation, Renwick Gallery, and a McDonald's. On the right were the White House grounds, the Eisenhower Executive Office Building, and Lafayette Square, all of which were surrounded by high black fencing that made a giant buffer zone around the White House.

He turned right on H Street NW. The intersection of H Street and 16th Street had become known as "Black Lives Matter Plaza." It was closed to traffic, especially today. People were gathered here,

---

4   The White House, "About the White House", 2024, https://www.whitehouse.gov/about-the-white-house/.

standing about on the road or sitting on the many barricades set up for crowd and traffic control. Many news cameras were set up on 16th Street, pointed south over BLM Plaza and the White House. Cameramen stood by, sitting on the barricades, smoking cigarettes. Reporters were in vans around the corner.

A white guy in his mid-thirties with long hair and skinny jeans stood playing folk songs on a guitar. His cell phone was recording him, transmitting to online viewers. It was mounted on a tripod on the cement barricade around St. John's Church. In the background, the camera caught the high black fence with the White House far in the distance behind, and the many signs and photos plastered to the fence. The signs were calls for justice. The photos were of men and women who were killed by the police—some in the streets, some while sleeping in their beds—for being black in America.

On the dirty sidewalk beside the fence around Lafayette Square sat a few old black men. They each wore white beards and woolen black berets, gazing out at the small groups of young people in the plaza. One of them watched as the white guy with long hair, skinny jeans, and guitar finished his performance, saying to his online audience:

> "Thanks everyone! I'll be in Baltimore
> tomorrow night and Charleston the
> next day! Please like and subscribe!"

He shut off the cell phone camera and put away his guitar. As he was leaving up 16th Street to head to Baltimore, two teenagers rode into the plaza on fixed-wheel bicycles. They did a few slow circles through the people standing around in the plaza, then rested the bikes against the barricade surrounding St. John's Church and took a seat. They were in the same place where the President had stood with the Bible months before, for a photo. They stayed a while to check out the quiet morning scene in the Plaza, like a farmer's market that had just begun. It was the morning of Election Day, 2020.

The windows of St. John's Church were boarded up, with black char marks around. The church had apparently burned recently. Up above it was another building, much larger and shinier than the church. It was the building of the largest federation of labor unions in America—the AFL-CIO.[5] Several big, tough-looking white guys were on the steps, glaring out at the people milling past in BLM Plaza. They looked very serious, with their arms across their chests, shaved heads, black polo

---

[5]   Wikipedia, s.v. "AFL-CIO", 2024, https://en.wikipedia. org/wiki/AFL-CIO.

shirts, and wrap-around sunglasses. In contrast to their hostile appearance was the sign above them, the largest in D.C., hung from the corner of the building, saying:

**AFL-CIO SUPPORTS
BLACK LIVES MATTER**

One of the two young guys got up to leave. He picked up his bike from against the barricade by St. John's Church, saying to the other while swinging his leg over the bike:

> "Let's come back later, when
> things get *crazy.*"

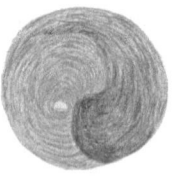

CHAPTER 5

The Dri-Mark Pen

It was a warm spring evening in Minneapolis. A forty-six-year-old black man walked into Cup Foods on 38th Street and Chicago Avenue to buy cigarettes. He paid for the cigarettes with a twenty, then left the store. The store owner—thinking the twenty was counterfeit—followed the man to his vehicle, demanding the cigarettes back. Apparently, the store did not have a Dri-Mark pen handy to check the bill during the sale of the cigarettes. There was some arguing. Then the police were called.

Four officers arrived. The customer of Cup Foods who bought the cigarettes, George Floyd, was detained and placed in handcuffs, face down on the ground. One of the officers, Derek Chauvin, then kneeled and pressed his knee into the back of Floyd's neck, bearing his full weight on it. The man on the ground, father of three and grandfather of two, began to cry out between gasps of air, begging for his life.

He called out weakly, "I can't breathe. I can't breathe."

As the moments dragged on, Chauvin looked up from time to time at cell phone cameras and people telling him to get off. The other officers stood by, frozen, or on guard, should bystanders attempt to intervene. Chauvin's eyes would then turn back downward, focusing on his knee on the man's neck on the ground. He was deeply focused, moving his head very slowly, like a snake strangling its prey, as if his actions demanded intense concentration.

At last, the paramedics arrived. They got out of the ambulance and saw what was happening, and immediately instructed Chauvin to get off the man, who now lay still on the ground.

As he finally stood, looking at what he had done, his face expressed the innocent look of a deer in headlights. He did not look so confident now. He looked scared. It was as though something had taken over him, as if his actions had not been within his control.

He thought to himself, "So long as the restraint was taught in the Academy, the restraint used was reasonable, yes?" Sure, he didn't cover his ass by yelling "Get BACK!" the whole time when applying force, but that was considered excusable, no?

He was just being a good boy, abiding by Rationalism, Pragmatism, and Common Sense— killing his own brother.

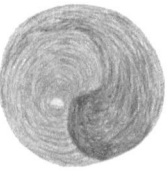

CHAPTER 6

The Leviathan

Gene stood on the back deck of the Stalwart, smoking a cigarette. The boat was tied alongside a massive oil barge called Barge 450-3, moored by Saw Island. On the charts, the buoy was called "Saw Island 5." The rocky shoreline was covered in snow. A deer was standing on the edge of the evergreen trees, emaciated, starving from little grass to eat in winter. Beyond Saw Island, two oil tankers were loading oil at the Valdez Marine Terminal. One was very low in the water, almost ready to depart. The waters of the bay were very calm, not a ripple in sight.

He put his foot up on the cap rail of the old tugboat and looked up at the mountains. Lines of blowing snow shot from the highest peaks, foretelling a coming wind. They quickly spread out into mare's tails in the steel-blue sky, lit brightly by the early setting sun. It would soon be bitterly cold. The steel decks of the tug would become encased in ice from the freezing spray. Fingers would freeze while trying to strike a match. The body's temperature would slowly fall to freezing, extinguishing life by exposure, if not prepared.

It is a "cold, cruel world" indeed, as his father used to warn him. To survive, one must "subdue" the Earth with those tools of the Brain—Rationalism, Pragmatism, and Common Sense—setting aside that burning, lofty idealism of the hopelessly romantic Heart, lest one starves like the helpless, emaciated deer on the shoreline in Alaska winter.

But when God told Adam and Eve to "subdue" the Earth—including even "the fowl of the air"— was it a command to be followed mindlessly without consideration of the ends?

> "And God blessed them, and God said
> unto them, Be fruitful, and multiply, and
> replenish the earth, *and subdue it*: and
> have dominion over the fish of the sea,
> and over the fowl of the air, and over every
> living thing that moveth upon the earth."[6]

---

[6] Genesis 1:28 (KJV).

The Europeans seemed to think so. At least, that is what they preached. They sailed the Earth in ships seeming to be moved by magic, systematically charting every square inch of all that there was to be subdued, wowing native peoples who stood on the shorelines where they landed, and subdued them too.

In subduing, they taught that to subdue was to please God. They taught that heathen-like passions of the Heart were Sin. They taught that to be "spiritual" was good—yes, sort of, but only in an abstract sense, *after* Life was over. Here, now, a direct, spiritual connection to one's existence—to the Earth, to all the Universe—could not be tolerated. This life, all Life, was a steppingstone to Heaven. That is all. To see it as something to behold in wonder and preserve forever was stupid.

Once the connection to Earth was severed, everything was for sale. Where it had been unthinkable to cut into the sacred Earth, the great Extraction began, with all the gold going back to the Motherland. The world we know came to be.

In 1845, Henry David Thoreau sought to reject this system, performing an "experiment" of living in solitude for two years and two months, to show just how little is needed to sustain a human existence. He left his mind free for romantic wanderings and attainment of the ideal. He did so beside a beautiful pond in New England, called Walden Pond.[7]

But of his "experiment," Thoreau conceded, "[it] is difficult to begin without borrowing[.]"[8] Indeed, he did not make nor own the tools he used to build his cabin, borrowing an axe to clear the land. He also did not make the materials for his cabin, but rather "bought the shanty of James Collins, an Irishman who worked on the Fitchburg Railroad, for boards."[9] Further, he was permitted to build his cabin on pristine land owned by his close friend and mentor, Ralph Waldo Emerson. Further yet, he did not just use a small piece of land by Walden Pond, but also "two acres and a-half of light and sandy soil near it" to plant beans.[10] Moreover, it was not as though Thoreau conducted his experiment of independence in the wilderness of Alaska. Rather, he was within walking distance of his family's home in Concord, Massachusetts. If he really needed something from civilization, he could easily get it.

He then spent two years in the woods, scorning the metaphorical railroad and train lumbering through the woods with its ugly "smoke and steam

---

[7] *See generally*, Thoreau, H.D., *Walden; or, Life in the Woods*, Boston, 1845, https://archive.org/stream/waldenor-li00thor/waldenorli00thor_djvu.txt.

[8] *Id.* at p. 34.

[9] *Id.* at p. 36.

[10] *Id.* at p. 46.

and hissing," and Rationalism, Pragmatism, and Common Sense—all that which allows mankind to "subdue" the Earth, proclaiming in a pretty poem, loudly and proudly (and in utter hypocrisy), that he would "never go" to see where the train ends:

> "What's the railroad to me?
> I never go to see
> Where it ends.
> It fills a few hollows,
> And makes banks for the swallows,
> It sets the sand a-blowing,
> And the blackberries a-growing,
> But I cross it like a cart-path in
> the woods. I will not have my eyes
> put out and my ears spoiled by its
> smoke and steam and hissing."[11]

With the philosophical problem of the railroad thus disregarded, Thoreau was then "free" to lose himself in romantic reverie, basking in the wild song of the free-spirited loon, writing the most influential book in American history, advising others to do the same.

Hence the Boomer Hippies—sold on Thoreau's hypocrisy, sold on flowery idealism, high on LSD—shunned all that impeded their hedonistic reverie.

---

[11] *See id.* at p. 108.

Like Thoreau living on another's land and using products of a system that he purported to reject for his comfort and happiness, the Boomers took the prosperous America handed to them on a silver platter as a given and spent a decade indulging in all the free time that such prosperity made possible. Then, they spent the decades after plundering it.

They ignored the Rule in the children's book *Tootle*, expressing the conservative viewpoints of their conservative parents of the 1950s:

"Stay on the Rails, No Matter What!"

That book is about a young freight train, Tootle, who was in school to become an industrious grown-up train pulling big, important things from city to city. But Tootle had a romantic bent. He wished to pursue the passions of his Heart first and foremost. The Rationalism, Pragmatism, and Common Sense of the guided rails impeded his wanted identity. Tootle thus went off the rails, racing the horse across the beautiful meadow, smelling the buttercups and making daisy chains, until finally caught. The whole community then helped to redirect the misguided young train back to the rails, where he belonged.[12]

---

[12] *See* Crampton, Gertrude. *Tootle*. New York: Golden Books Publishing Co., 1945.

Like Tootle in the meadow, and like Thoreau beside his pond, the Boomer Hippies spent the 1960s in rejection of any sort of structured, conservative thinking. When the 1960s ended, however, the Boomer Hippies needed no red flags waving to get them back on the tracks. They saw their friends, one by one, dropping off like flies. They were taking positions of security in the "apparatus" they had rejected, abandoning their hopes of ever reconciling all those idealistic notions of Life with the "cold, cruel world" they faced. They quickly learned to use the "apparatus" they had condemned to plunder all the opportunity handed to them—their time off the rails was soon nothing more than a poignant memory.

Gene refused to accept as reality the meaningless decades following Boomer Hippies' hedonistic, morally cloaked and drug-infused reverie. He sought to vindicate all that high-minded idealism of Henry David Thoreau that inspired them. He would not run to a pond on someone else's land, but would conduct his version of Thoreau's "experiment" in the most excruciating way possible—getting to Walden Pond by a 4,817 mile walk in Hell, facing the Devil in the Steam Engine.

The stillness of the water beside the tugboat where Gene stood smoking suddenly broke. A giant whale rose from below. Its back, covered with barnacles, took several seconds to arch over the surface. The tail finally rose, curving against the backdrop of snow-covered mountains, droplets of water falling off and dripping into the still bay. Finally, it sank into the deep. The giant animal's smell permeated the air long after it was gone.

It did not spout. It did not breathe. Swimming at full speed, it was on the hunt.

Gene looked up again at the streaks of white shooting from the mountains, then at the still-boiling waters where the Leviathan sank, tossing his finished cigarette.

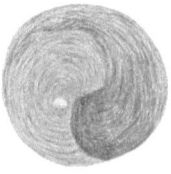

CHAPTER 7

The Square

Three large black men stood on the sidewalk beside Farragut Square, talking quietly. They wore heavy black coats and full-brimmed, black hats. At intervals, their talking rose into moments of laughter that resonated in the quiet. The vapor from their breath hung long in the cold, still air of downtown Washington D.C.

All the buildings around the square were covered with wooden boards. An old Chinese lady peered out momentarily from the boarded doorway of her shop as she closed for the night. It was November 3, 2020, almost midnight.

Sounds began to echo between the buildings from commotion blocks away. The sounds were booms of explosions, and the voices were of a crowd, rising and falling intermittently.

Moments later, black silhouettes poured into the dark streets surrounding Farragut Square. They were protestors and police. The protestors wore black, with black umbrellas held before them. The police wore black uniforms, black armor, black helmets, and black shields. A voice from the protestors led the crowd in chanting:

"What do we want?
JUSTICE!
When do we want it?
NOW!"

A line quickly formed between protestors and police. There was scuffling. The police grabbed a girl as she screamed, placing her in handcuffs and pulling her into a waiting van. The police had a megaphone too, countering the chants of the protestors with the continuously repeated command:

"Get BACK!
Get BACK!
Get BACK!"

A new voice took to the megaphone of the protestors. This voice was not leading a new chant, but seemed to express the sentiment of all in the crowd that night:

"I'm fucking TIRED of being told to 'GET
BACK!' I'm FUCKING TIRED of being
FUCKING TOLD to 'GET BACK!'"

There were loud booming sounds as flash bang
and sting ball grenades exploded, lighting up the
walls of buildings around the square. Then, the
crowd abruptly dispersed through Farragut Square.
Through facial coverings, masks, and goggles, their
eyes showed a grave sense of their purpose.

Soon, all was quiet again, save an alarm
somewhere that buzzed continuously, and the
voices of the three large black men talking beside
the square, in full-brimmed hats and heavy black
coats, the vapor from their breath hanging long in
the cold, still air of D.C.

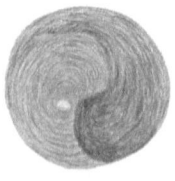

The Pursuit

The grassland sank down to a ravine. He climbed down through the thick trees and bushes. At the bottom was a small stream. He kneeled, drank heavily, and splashed some water on his face and chest. His eyes then fixed upon something across the stream.

She was reaching her delicate hands into the water. Her long eyelashes covered her downward-looking eyes. Her silky black hair fell around her shoulders and breasts. Her appearance was soft and flowing. An unknown feeling swept over him.

She looked up, then immediately rose and disappeared. He stood, staring at the place where she had gone. Instinctively, he crossed the stream and followed her into the dense trees. He saw her hair flashing momentarily in a beam of sunlight, then disappearing again—then he stopped.

There was a man standing before him. His powerful arms were held across his broad chest. He had gray hair and dark, well-aged skin. On his face were geometric shapes, accentuating the fierce look in his eyes. The whites of his eyes stood out brightly against the darkness of the canopy.

Now finding himself an intruder, he felt another instinct and slowly took a step backward. He paused for a moment, looking searchingly into the eyes of the old warrior who stared back, expressionless. Finally, he turned to go. He went back across the stream, out of the ravine, up to the open grassland.

The Sun set and it grew dark as he walked slowly through the silver sea of grass. The air was still. Crickets were chirping and the stars shimmered in the sky above. He looked up at the stars, thinking of the Nymph in the ravine. At last, he lay down to sleep.

In his sleep, under the expansive Universe above him, there were visions of naked bodies, entangled and moving, rubbing and gripping each other. Eyes were closed and lips parted in ecstasy. There was moaning and crying, the sounds of procreation, women bearing children, babies taking their first breaths, and of the sick and old, dropping off. It was Life making Life, continuously and forever—but to die eventually, as Life is supposed to. But it was here, now, in all its mad wonder. It was, it seemed, the consciousness of the Universe, the eye of the heavens, the mind to wonder at its own existence.

Then a voice began to shout, "Wake up!"

A bright light flashed across his eyelids. He was being shaken violently. He struggled to wake up. The voice shouted again, "We need you outside!"

Finally, his eyes opened. The shaking and shouting ceased. The bright light was gone. He clicked on the reading light and swung his legs over the side of the bed, pulling on his pants and work boots to go outside.

The surface of the water was covered by a thick blanket of snow floating on top. The tugboat moved along slowly, parting and pushing it aside. On the foredeck were two others, leaned up against the thick, steel cap rails at the tip of the bulwarks with giant tires chained to the outside. Huge, orange ropes lay on the deck. Lights shimmered in the distance over the bow of the tug—two white lights, one over the other, and a green light below—a ship, moving slowly along in the blackness.

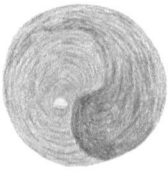

CHAPTER 9

The Stage

Gene sat on a bench in Farragut Square, sipping black coffee from 7-Eleven, reading news, writing, thinking, soaking in the warmth of the Sun after the freezing night. He also worked on making a sign on a piece of cardboard, with a large, black, felt-tip pen.

The news played the incumbent president, who had been up in the middle of the night announcing he had won the election, though votes were still being counted:

> "We want all voting to stop. We don't
> want them to find any ballots at four
> o'clock in the morning and add them to
> the list. Okay? It's a very sad moment.

> And we will win this. And as far as I'm
> concerned, we already have won."[13]

Republican senators fell in line. Senator Lindsey Graham ominously announced on November 5th that, on the following Saturday, all Senate Republicans would be going to the White House to get "the story" that (Graham admonished) *all* Senate Republicans were to go out and spread.

Gene thought these statements from American politicians sounded like the kind of double-speak one would expect to hear from officials in a country like Belarus—Europe's last dictatorship. Just before the U.S. presidential election in 2020, Belarusians demanded a return to democracy, with horrible results. Lukashenko had become the first president of Belarus in 1994, after the fall of the Soviet Union. He won on a populist platform, proclaiming:

> "I am neither with the leftists nor the
> rightists, but with the people against
> those who rob and deceive them."[14]

---

[13] "President Donald Trump attempts to claim election victory as several states still count ballots." 2020. YouTube video, 9:18, posted by CNBC Television, November 4, 2020, https://www.youtube.com/watch?v=W9d6j2uO6MI.

[14] Filtenborg, Emil; Weichert, Stefan, "'He stopped listening... and became cruel': Lukashenko remembered by former campaign manager," Euro News, September 24, 2020 (updated September 28, 2020), https://www.

Once elected, however, the populist base that was responsible for Lukashenko's victory in 1994 soon realized that Lukashenko was only "with" himself. In 2020, they demanded a return to democratic government and free elections, but Lukashenko declined. Instead, he arrested opposition activists, protesters, journalists, and bloggers. There were hundreds of documented cases of torture, sexual abuse, and rape. Poll documents were falsified in favor of Lukashenko. His opponent was forced to flee the country. The United States declared the election a sham.

Gene wondered, if this type of system came to America, what would become of fundamental rights Americans have known and taken for granted—like the right to procedural due process, much less any "substantive" due process, and even enumerated rights like freedom of speech and freedom of the press? What would become of BLM?

This further begged the question: when were the Boomer Hippies finally going to adhere to what they proclaimed was their duty, so heatedly from their university campuses in the 1960s?

---

euronews.com/my-europe/2020/09/24/he-stopped-listening-and-became-cruel-lukashenko-remembered-by-former-campaign-manager.

"There is a time when the operation of
the machine becomes so odious, makes
you so sick at heart, that you can't take
part! You can't even passively take part!
And you've got to put your bodies
upon the gears and upon the wheels ...
upon the levers, *upon all the apparatus,*
and you've got to make it stop!"[15]

Looking around D.C., it appeared they were not going to adhere to this at all. The Boomer Hippies had already had their fun. Watching the democracy that had given them everything finally fall was a fitting end to the Baby Boomers' utter, loud-and-proud hypocrisy. They were spending their twilight years collecting social security while it was still funded and going to doctor visits paid for by Medicare, sitting in their hybrid cars at the Starbucks drive-thru, listening to NPR with feigned concern, finding it all very interesting, getting ready to fly to Iceland to go kayaking, getting in touch with nature like Thoreau, choosing flights with fewer legs, paying extra "to be green."

A gentleman in a suit walked through Farragut Square. He stopped and looked at the sign Gene was making on a piece of cardboard he had found, with

---

[15]   Mario Savio, "Bodies Upon the Gears" address given at Sproul Hall, University of California, Berkeley, December 2, 1964.

the thick permanent marker. The man then pulled two dollars from his wallet and handed it to Gene.

"No," Gene said, "you should give this to someone else."

The gentleman responded, "No, I think I want to give it to you."

"Hm," Gene thought, as he watched the stranger walk away.

Late in the afternoon, a camera crew of three appeared in the middle of the square. They spoke in a foreign language, sounding eastern European. The reporter was very pretty, well-dressed and well-made-up with black hair and a thick, red jacket made of wool. They waited a while, the cameramen smoking cigarettes. Then, two young black guys appeared and joined them. The lady spoke to them in her thick accent. She then handed each a brand new, bright red hat that said:

"MAKE AMERICA GREAT AGAIN"

Then all of them went off walking together, heading toward BLM Plaza. The two black guys walked ahead, with the red "MAGA" hats on their heads. The film crew and reporter trailed behind, filming.

A little while later, Gene looked up to see the two young black guys pass back through Farragut Square, no longer followed by the film crew, no longer wearing the red MAGA hats, and with uneasy looks on their faces about what they had just done.

In the evening, Gene walked to BLM Plaza. He bought a T-shirt from a few young black guys selling them from a folding table for twenty dollars each. The T-shirts were solid black, with a tiny shape of the American continent right over the heart, in red—a symbol of love for country. Bold words across the front, in green font, said:

"MAKE AMERICA LAUGH AGAIN"

Down the street, small groups of young people stood and socialized in the middle of the plaza. An old white guy stood on a concrete barricade above them, waving his arms and yelling, shouting about different conspiracies he knew about. The onlookers stood below, laughing, passing joints, and encouraging him to go on.

The old black men were still sitting on the sidewalk with their woolen berets, looking out at the small crowds. Next to them, a boom box also sat on the sidewalk, playing a political protest song. It had extensive, poetic lyrics about social problems and unity among Americans of all colors, and a chorus that repeated a blunt message regarding the incumbent president.

A white guy rode in little circles on a bicycle in the middle of the plaza, talking quietly through a megaphone, saying:

"Go home, Trump. Donald
Trump, go home."

A large black guy with long black braids rode into the plaza on a big motor scooter. He drove around the small groups, revving the engine very loudly, splitting the quiet of the plaza. The guy who was riding on the fixed-wheel bicycle doing circles with the bullhorn moved a bit further away. Finally, he stopped, and the horrible noise ceased. He got off and joined his friends, and the quiet of before resumed.

A group of tall white guys stood by in a small circle. They all had the word "PRESS" emblazoned on their jackets and were sharing a six pack of beer, talking, laughing, and bullshitting with each other.

Suddenly, the sound of helicopters suddenly filled the cold evening. The tall white guys with PRESS on their jackets quickly finished their beers and rushed off to where the helicopter spotlight shined down up the street.

There did not seem to be anything happening warranting police presence, but a brigade of Metropolitan Police Department officers soon arrived on bicycles, apparently from their base a block or two away. At their base were dozens and dozens of police cars, police riot vehicles, etc.—despite calls for defunding of police departments in 2020.

The police formed a line across the street, holding their bicycles between them and a small crowd of people close by. News cameras on 16th Street turned to film, broadcasting the commotion to news channels around the world. The small crowd that had been standing and socializing suddenly began chanting angrily and forcing itself against the line of police officers.

The police arrested a person from the crowd, then left just as quickly as they had arrived. The helicopter overhead disappeared. The quiet of the plaza returned. The young people hanging around the plaza resumed their socializing.

Later, around midnight, a tall, lanky black guy walked hurriedly down 16th, screaming at the top of his lungs at the people quietly standing around the plaza, "Y'all a bunch of fucking hypocrites! I been here every day since George Floyd died!"

But if he was there every day, it was just for exercise. He continued without stopping, turning the corner by St. John's church and quickly disappearing beneath the dark row of maple trees behind the White House. Gene turned his head to see a cameraman following the screaming man, lowering his camera from his shoulder and turning the corner by the church. He, too, disappeared down the dark row of maple trees behind the White House.

A girl in the plaza said quietly to her friends, "What's that guy's problem?"

CHAPTER 10

The Stowaway

Gene was taking a class called "Hazardous Waste Operations and Emergency Response." It was under the Ballard Bridge, in Seattle, next to the Inland Boatman's Union offices. He had signed up with the union over the past couple of months, completing drug and medical tests and many required forms.

The union told Gene he would need the class for any tugboat outfit he might apply for. So, Gene signed up for the class in Seattle, with a bunch of onery looking tugboat men, feeling very out of place. While on a break, he walked the docks outside, looking at all the nets on the fishing boats readying to go to Alaska. His phone began to ring.

It was the dispatcher from a tugboat company, called "Crowley Marine Services." Crowley got

Gene's phone number through the union. The female dispatcher asked if Gene would work as a cook. Gene did not know how to cook. He fumbled at first, but of course, he then quickly said, yes, of course I will cook!

Gene had caught on.

He made his way to the sea of shipping containers and gantry cranes of many bright colors under the West Seattle Bridge—Harbor Island—with the emerald buildings of downtown Seattle across the water in the distance. He found a pier where many hulking tugboats were tied up, then climbed aboard the Sea Voyager.

There were engineers working on the hydraulic tow pins on the stern of the tug. They were all very greasy. "Come here and put some grease on that shirt!" one yelled, seeing Gene's bright red "Coca-Cola" T-shirt he had bought at Salvation Army the day prior.

Gene put his bags in his stateroom and climbed the three decks of the old tugboat to the wheelhouse to sign in with the mate on watch. Then he went back down to the galley to survey the situation. The galley was filthy after months in the shipyard. He did some cleaning. Then, the mate came down from the wheelhouse, saying, "Stores are here."

Minutes later, a refrigerator truck arrived on the dock. The engineer fired up the crane and lifted four pallets of food onto the back deck of the tug, each stacked seven feet high and wrapped tightly in shrink wrap.

Soon a chain of guys was bringing stores into the galley—silently, like a machine, placing the items on every surface for Gene to contend with.

He scrambled to make order of chaos. He cleaned more, then opened dozens of boxes of food for weeks at sea and put things away, creating some semblance of a system of organization. He used the helpful photos in the *Better Home and Garden Cookbook* to identify large, frozen cuts of unknown parts of different animals, labeling them with a black felt marker as they went into the huge, commercial-grade freezers.

In the middle of all of this, the mate came down from the wheelhouse again, telling Gene to head outside to help with work on deck. Gene put on a hard hat and went outside.

Three huge lines connected the tugboat to the barge. The stevedores let go of the lines and the tug moved the barge slowly away from the dock. When the tug and barge were clear of the dock, the three barge lines were loosened and the deckhand on the barge lifted the huge eyes off each bitt, one by one, before scurrying down the pigeonholes on the side of the barge and over the huge tires on the side of the tug.

He then went to the back deck with a hammer to trip the pelican hook that held thousands and thousands of pounds of towing gear on deck. Keeping his distance, the deckhand reached out and hit the ring holding the hook closed, then ran away as fast as possible. Thousands of pounds of chain and giant shackles raced between the towing pins in a blur of rusty dust. The huge chain slammed against the tow pin when all the gear was overboard, and the captain began turning the tugboat in front of the barge. The barge was towering above the stern of the tug, reverberating hollow, echoing sounds like temple bells. The engineer stood by the captain, operating the controls for the tow winch, paying out the two-and-a-half-inch wire little by little.

On the trip north, the engineer spent a good deal of time in the galley, standing by the counter where Gene worked furiously, doing a great deal of bullshitting. Gene was starting to get a handle on the job, following the cookbook and working fourteen hours a day. The guys of the crew who had grumbled with looks of dread at the first awful meal were soon eating like kings. The engineer lived in a house he built with an armory of weapons. He said he liked to always keep about 50,000 rounds of ammunition on hand, just in case. He kept his gray hair slicked back and always smelled of fresh aftershave. He was a Boomer, but no hippie. He told many stories of his life spent keeping rusty tugboats afloat and going across the Pacific Ocean, towing multiple barges. He also talked about memories of his time off work, driving hot rods down the main strip of his hometown in the 1980s.

Gene and the engineer seemed an unlikely pair to hit it off so well, with the engineer being a staunch conservative and Gene not hiding his affinity for Country Joe and the Fish, which he frequently played in the galley where he worked. But they did.

The engineer was a big reader, telling Gene all about Leo Tolstoy's *War and Peace*—about old Pierre, reconciling that which can't be reconciled with alcohol—and Victor Hugo's *Les Misérables*, saying of that one in his gravelly voice, "That's a *great* piece of fucking literature."

They talked about the stereotypical liberal, sitting in a coffee shop, reading *The New Yorker,* scorning that which is necessary for their fragile existence, ignoring the unpleasant details of life, avoiding the type of thinking not conducive to "wellness," "mindfulness," and "spirituality," who then "get in their electric vehicle and go get an abortion," like Kellyanne Conway said. The engineer would respond to such sentiment by leaning forward over the counter toward Gene, saying, syllable by syllable, *"Ex-act-ly!"*

One morning, Gene saw land out of the small circular porthole in the galley. He went out through the winch room to look.

The barge was following close behind now, the tow wire shortened. They were sailing up a narrow, magical, mystical, majestic fjord. Steep mountains rose on both sides, still capped with snow in mid-summer. In the crevices of the mountains, azure glaciers poured down. A bald eagle flew in the steely sky overhead. The air was cool and easy to breathe, scented with pollen from the evergreen trees on the shore. They were in Alaska.

CHAPTER 11

The Glow

His eyes opened. A small bird landed on a long blade of grass. The grass bent over. Another landed on the same blade, and the grass bent lower. Then another landed, and another, and another, until the long green blade bent so far that birds nearer to the end began to slide and fall off. Suddenly, all flew away at once, and the grass stood up high again.

A tiny mouse ran past, stopped for a moment to look at something in the dirt, then disappeared into a hole in the ground.

Overhead in the sky were bands of light, colored like the rainbow—red, orange, yellow, green, blue, indigo, and violet—where the last darkness of the night was setting.

He stood, rubbing his eyes of sleep, stretched his arms in circles a few times, then began moving again. He knew nothing of existence but an urge to keep moving, and of thoughts of the Nymph in the ravine, and of thoughts of the old warrior's judging eyes who had stood in his path.

He went west, always west, where the Moon set. The horizon stayed the same—an ever-continuing line of yellow against the sky. But today, the landscape changed.

In the strange bodies of watery light on the horizon, there was a place where the plain rose to a high plateau. Puffy white clouds hung over it in an otherwise cloudless sky.

The Sun set. It grew dark again. He was climbing now, up the plateau, breathing hard as he did, anxious to get a better vantage. At last, the ground became level. He stood at the top, turning slowly, scanning the sweeping view—then stopped at a strange sight.

Over the horizon were thin lines of white meandering into the sky. They were lit from below by orange, glowing light. Catching his breath, very tired from the climb, he sat down against a rock and watched this mysterious sight. He was anxious to keep moving, to see what this was, but he was also exhausted, and it was dark. He sat against the rock, watching the stars falling, one by one, setting into the orange, glowing light over the horizon. His eyelids grew heavy, and he fell to sleep in the cool air high above the plain.

Traveling all through the next day, down the plateau and further west into the night again, he came to the source of the orange, glowing light on the horizon. He stood a little distance off, watching. There were others, like him, around a fire—appearing as silhouettes that moved like the flames themselves, dancing to the beating of drums, overlayed with the haunting voices of women singing in maniacal joy. One of the younger women was the Nymph from the ravine.

Searching, he met eyes with the old warrior, his face still covered with geometric tattoos—a pillar of Rationalism, Pragmatism, and Common Sense.

Under the light of the Moon, away from the fire, the old warrior asked, "What have you got to offer?"

The wanderer glanced over at the nymph dancing beside the fire, then once more into the fierce eyes of the old warrior.

He smiled, bowed low, then turned to go.

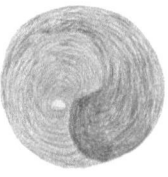

CHAPTER 12

The Coffee Shop

The coffee in front of Gene had a foam of very tiny bubbles on top—white in the middle and brown on the sides—in the shape of a heart. The skilled barista had made it only moments before. The tiny bubbles reflected the lights in the shop, popping and releasing bits of steam. The cup had a brown sleeve which said:

> "Made with 97 Percent Post-
> Consumer Recycled Products."

It was sunny outside, but Gene wore a warm jacket in the shop. He got very cold, being in his office all day, from the air conditioning. Some of the secretaries even had space heaters, although that was against fire regulations. The coffee shop was also cold.

People sat at wooden tables, looking at their phones. Other people entered, all holding cell phones. Most got their coffee and left immediately, looking up only to order.

There were two baristas behind the counter, one male with hair pulled back in a tight bun, the other female with purple hair and a nose ring. When a customer approached, the male barista would give the customer a quick look as he moved continuously, asking, "What can I brew you?"

The customers did not look at the barista much, either. They were only there for a quick transaction before resuming looking at their phones. After ordering, they held plastic cards over a little screen on the counter to pay.

The female barista suddenly yelled, "Tall skinny latte for Jennifer!"

A girl in yoga pants looked up from her phone and stepped up to the counter, taking her coffee and leaving out the door.

The lights in the shop were dim and relaxing, hanging from wires on the black ceiling. But music played very loudly over speakers mounted on the walls, apparently so customers would seek quiet elsewhere. The song that was playing had a woman singing, her voice resembling the last meows of a dying cat.

Food items were on display behind glass, each wrapped in plastic with labels in earthy colors—tiny croissants, cookies, and cakes, pink and blue balls on wooden sticks, sandwiches with sausage and egg— all of which looked like they were made of plastic, not digestible food. The line for customers was framed by low shelves and wicker baskets holding dusty bags of ground coffee and hard plastic cups for purchase.

Gene had to get back to the office for a teleconference, but he was still sitting at the table, staring at the small, glowing, LED light hanging over the table. It was blinding when looked at directly. Still, he looked. Something perplexed him about the light. It seemed that up the wire something was moving inside. He followed it with his eyes as it went through the conduit on the ceiling to the wall, where it joined other wires, finally disappearing somewhere outside the shop. He thought, "What … was that?"

He shook himself, suddenly conscious of how he must look. He stood, rubbing a green spot out of his eyes, and quickly headed for the door. He disappeared into the people rushing past on the dirty city sidewalk outside.

Tiny bubbles continued to pop in the cup of coffee on the table, releasing bits of steam, lit by the LED lights hanging from the ceiling above.

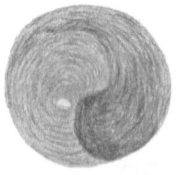

CHAPTER 13

The Theory

Gene returned to the office for the call with a client.

"Fuck," he thought, "where's my coffee?"

As Gene hung up the phone afterward, a partner of the firm appeared in the doorway of his office. Gene and this partner often spent hours of the workday together, talking and sometimes also strategizing cases. The partner had many stories to tell of his time as a prosecutor. Today, however, Gene's thoughts wandered.

Outside the window, the tops of trees blew around in the wind. Beneath the window was a bookshelf filled with dusty books of codes and regulations, which Gene had covered with large tapestries and potted plants. On the other side of the office was another shelf with many things on it that had no other place to go. In a frame on the shelf was a photo of a beautiful young mother, sitting on the floor and against the wall of an old cottage by the sea, looking relaxed and at ease. In her arms was a baby bundled in clothes for sleeping. The baby stared intently at the camera as her tiny fingers curled greedily around the bottle of warm milk that she drank from. On the wall above the shelf were many drawings in pearl-colored crayons. Gene gazed for a while at the drawing of a surreal rainbow that hung low over a round, green hill.

On his desk was a yellow legal pad with start and stop times for different cases he was working on. There was a computer mouse and keyboard, and two huge monitors with dozens of sticky notes. The computer screens showed open emails, PDFs, and Word documents.

Then, something snapped Gene from daydreaming: the partner said, "If your theory is going to succeed, it has to encompass *all* the facts."

As the partner's story continued, Gene thought of these words, and of the LED lights back in the coffee shop, hanging from black wires on the ceiling, leading to somewhere outside.

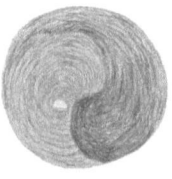

CHAPTER 14

The Ovation

Gene arrived at Anchorage Airport once again, joining thousands who came from around the United States to rotate into long shifts of work in the oil, mining, and fishing industries, stepping off red-eye flights with looks of dread under their camouflage hats, wearing work clothes and heavy jackets, hunkering down in the small terminal filled with Jet-A exhaust fumes, trying to catch a nap with horribly out-of-place synthetic music by The Beatles playing over speakers from the ceiling, interrupted at intervals by airport security announcements.

In their dreams they dreamed flowery, far-out, nonsensical things, connecting with uninhibited, passionate wonder before their alarms went off to get on small airplanes to the far reaches of Alaska, holding black coffees from the airport Starbucks cart as they boarded, once again going to face all the Rationalism, Pragmatism, and Common Sense necessary to achieve the fatalistic and unquestioned pursuits of Man.

Then, weeks or months later, they came back through Anchorage Airport on their way home, freed at last from the drudgery, often stopping at the Chili's Restaurant bar, chatting with other workers sitting beside them while using alcohol to put some bright colors in their eyes, in protest of common sense, the expeditious route to something that feels like "wellness," "mindfulness," and "spirituality" after so much banality, paid for with hard-earned wages and a headache, soon circling around to face it again.

Gene boarded a plane for Dead Horse, filled with many workers going to man the oil fields of the North Slope. It flew over Alyeska Range, then the Brooks Range, landing finally in Dead Horse. Outside the small airport was a white pickup truck waiting to get Gene.

They headed out on an artificial road raised very high above the tundra. There were miles and miles and miles of huge oil pipelines set up high on pilings above the tundra, so that caribou could walk underneath them. They passed by giant pump stations, towers with huge flames rising, power stations, giant trailers, portable crew quarters the size of hotels, seas of white pickup trucks with the names of oil companies on them, and an arctic fox flashing white running across the lumpy tundra.

The truck pulled over to allow space for a truck three times larger than your normal eighteen-wheel semi-truck. It was pulling a massive piece of drilling equipment on its giant bed, to be installed out there on the tundra, slowly rising to the Brooks Range in the south. A herd of mosquito-bitten caribou stumbled by soon after, making them wait again.

At last, they made it out to the gloomy, artificial spit of land where the base of Crowley's operations on the North Slope, "Barge 218," lay up against the beach, held by two huge anchors. Gene climbed the gangway.

There was a "bear gate" at the entrance of the barge, to keep polar bears out. Gene went through the bear gate and stepped onto the barge. CONEX boxes were stacked two-high all over the barge, inside of which were welding and other shops, and storage for every kind of tool that may be needed far from civilization, and crew quarters, and a galley, and an office. He opened the door to check in the one with an office and found Carol. He asked her if the *Kalluk* had arrived.

"It certainly has." She pointed outside the window.

In the distance, the *Kalluk* was resting on wood blocks on the bleak, windswept, artificial spit of land, sheets of filthy plastic blowing from it in the wind. It was not a tugboat, but rather a crew boat

Crowley bought in Port Angeles, Washington, then shipped from Seattle to Alaska on a barge, then up the Dalton Highway by semi-truck, finally to Prudhoe Bay. It was to be used for quick transport of cargo and crew, and other things too.

Gene was a deckhand, working on becoming licensed as a mate, not an engineer. But he (and another Crowley deckhand who would be arriving soon) were supposed to fake it for the summer, acting as "engineers" of the *Kalluk*. The first task was to pull all the equipment they had removed weeks prior, in Seattle, and reinstall it, starting with the engine propulsion drives that connected to two Volvo Penta diesels.

But the other deckhand/engineer had not arrived yet, so the first day was spent rolling a barge down the road. Down the spit a way was a huge, 200-foot, black steel barge rolling ever so slowly on what looked like giant Tootsie Rolls. A bulldozer drove in front of the barge to pull it, and another bulldozer was behind, to brake. There was also a "Zoom Boom" that dragged the Tootsie Rolls from the back of the barge to the front with chains and shackles, to be rolled under the barge again, sliding around on the gravel banks of the raised artificial road.

It was not that hard to learn what to do. Guys with hardhats walked along in front of the barge, pushing and rolling in front of them one of the giant Tootsie Rolls. The guys spoke about what they usually do when engaged with such mindless preoccupation.

For a moment, there was a collective feeling that the bow of the barge was about to tip over and crush everyone—the Tootsie Roll being rolled would be let go, and the guys had to step aside quickly so they did not get rolled over. It took the rest of the day and half the next to get the barge rolled where it needed to go, a mile or so down the road. Gene never saw how the barge was finally put in the water without dragging the bulldozer too. The next day, he and the other deckhand/engineer were putting the *Kalluk* engines back together. They were proud, or rather amazed, when a day or two later the *Kalluk* was running again, flying across the waters of the Arctic Ocean.

Down the coast several hours was Point Oliktok, where there were several artificial islands offshore, each with many giant drill rigs on them. The islands were made of giant, white sandbags that looked just like a polar bear sleeping—which, coincidentally, gave real polar bears perfect camouflage.

More drill rigs and other huge modules were to be brought ashore in that summer's "heavy-lift" season—when the ocean is not frozen and new equipment is brought up to the oil fields by barge. Before the giant heavy-lift modules and drill rigs can be rolled off the barge, the barge must be sunk to the bottom. This was done by filling the voids with water. However, before the barge can be sunk, the bottom of the sea must be flat, so that the barge does not break under uneven distribution of weight. "Screeding" is the process of *hoʻolahalaha*—flattening—the ocean bottom in preparation for this.

The machines that were in use in the "screeding" process included the barge that had rolled down the road with a huge piece of steel welded to the front, with holes in it for water to flow through. This piece slid up and down in guides on the bow of the barge. There was also a giant forklift to raise and lower the "screed" in the steel guides, and two shallow-draft tugboats, belching black smoke all through the night, moving the barge around as it scraped the bottom.

There was concern from environmentalists that clouds of silt from this operation might disturb wildlife. So, the *Kalluk* was to put out and maintain "boom"—a floating curtain designed to catch things on the water's surface. They did this all night long, most nights, replacing broken boom, setting anchors—catching wet dust to protect the environment—working next to a platform of drill rigs with flames looking like a scene of the apocalypse. It satisfied the environmentalists and let the heavy lifts of that summer be completed.

It was a small part of a gigantic, collective effort of bringing a couple of drill rigs from Mobile,

Alabama (or wherever) to the frozen tundra north of the Arctic Circle, where polar bears with their cubs roamed the desolate spits of beach in the distance, to be used in drilling down seven miles into the Earth and puncturing oceans of oil, the stored light of millions of years of the Sun shining upon the Earth, which is then drawn up through well heads and sent through treatment plants, fourteen giant pump stations, down 800 miles of pipeline, over the Brooks Range and the Alyeska Range, winding finally into the fjord of Port Valdez to giant tanks on the shoreline, then pumped onto ships a million barrels at a time, heaved around by tugboats, then carried through hurricane-force storms of the Gulf of Alaska, with inert gases filling the voids to prevent explosions, then finally passing under the Golden Gate Bridge—with tourists gazing down from above at the romance of the passing ship and fog horns blowing a mournful cry and yachtsmen coming out of Sausalito, steering away—then to more bleak parts of the Bay, where it heated, treated, and separated into various petroleum products, then shipped to more waiting tanks around the country. At last, it is consumed, as a young woman with her car parked in the wrong direction at the gas station yanks the fuel hose across the hood of her car and squeezes the nozzle to fill the tank, with tears filling her eyes, before getting into the car again and stepping on the gas, heading to the gym—trying to devote a little time to her wellness, mindfulness, and spirituality—before going to one of her several jobs, which, combined, barely pay the bills, as the cars at the Indianapolis 500 race across the finish line and the crowd rises in uproarious applause at how well we monkeys have subdued the Earth with our Rationalism, Pragmatism, and Common Sense.

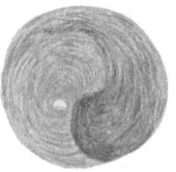

CHAPTER 15

The Nest

Gene noticed a few random bits of soft fern leaves around his doorstep. He was puzzled, as there were no ferns nearby. He looked around to investigate. On a couple flimsy leaves of a small tree just outside the door, the beginnings of a nest were forming.

Then, a small bird appeared. It was a very beautiful, light yellowish-green bird. She added a piece of grass to the nest she was making, then flew off again. Over the next few days, she primped the inside and outside of the nest until it was soft and insulated, busy from morning to night.

When finished, she got in and sat, day and night, riding in the delicate hammock tied to two flimsy leaves as it blew around wildly in the breeze. She did not worry that the leaves might fall off; she did not worry that the gardener might come and raise the gas-powered blower up a little too high; she did not worry about tomorrow's food, or global warming, or authoritarianism, or nuclear war, or artificial intelligence getting out of control. She just stayed in her little hammock, completely confident in the way her time was spent.

Gene had expected that the whole process of making new baby birds would take longer—i.e., that she would achieve her career objectives, pay off her student loans, travel to foreign countries, fulfill her "bucket" list, and reach a certain level of financial independence before she would settle down and begin thinking about babies. He expected that a male bird would appear and that there would be arguments about which religion the babies would be raised in, that there would be a big wedding with relatives and gifts, and much shopping for things to fill the nest.

But there was none of that. A day or two later, she was very still for a long time. During this time, her beak was open very wide. Her little white googly eyes with black dots in the middle seemed to be staring into the infinite. She was laying her eggs.

Gene saw her out of the nest finally, perched on the metal rail of the front step, looking light and airy and very pretty, cleaning her tiny feathers. She then flew off, soon to return. He cracked the door.

In the tiny nest were four tiny eggs.

Days later, the nest was filled with baby birds. Each time the mother returned and landed on the small leaves, the babies' heads snapped up with mouths wide open, shaking and quivering, desperate for nourishment, their eyes still covered with skin. When she flew off, the tiny heads would immediately fall to sleeping, the four beaks fitting together in a perfect octagon. She came and went all day, feeding her babies.

A second adult appeared, also bringing things to the nest. The boy bird had come to help.

The skinless baby birds quickly grew soft feathers of silky green. The nest was hanging by threads, loaded with birds, with barely enough room for the mother to sit on top.

The next day, the birds were gone, and the gardener came and blew the nest away.

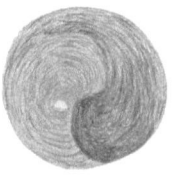

CHAPTER 16

The Pond

It was 5:45 a.m., still dark outside. Thirteen cars were lined up at the Starbucks drive-thru. Gene pulled into the upper parking lot outside Ross Dress for Less. He put on his rain gear then headed downstairs to the entrance of Whole Foods.

He typed in the code to enter, then walked down the aisles of kombucha to the back of the store and clicked on the heaters for the rotisserie chicken display. He clocked in, then went through the swinging doors to the back of the house of the prepared foods department.

He opened the refrigerator to check how many boxes of chickens were left—just one. He grabbed a cart and headed to the larger refrigerator at the other side of the store. In the refrigerator was another employee, dressed in a winter coat and making notes on paper. She worked in the refrigerators or freezers all day, making pre-made salads and other things in small plastic boxes, since the self-serve bar had been shut down for the pandemic. From time to time, she appeared by the dish pit to stand by the stove and hot ovens, to warm herself up.

Back through the swinging doors, he put one of the boxes on the counter and the rest in the smaller fridge. He then opened the box and quickly skewered the twelve dead chickens, two on each metal spike, keeping his lips closed tightly to avoid chicken juice splattering into his mouth. He then sprinkled some seasoning on them, cleaned the area, and carted everything through the swinging doors.

After starting the rotisserie, he went back through the doors to the dish pit. A song by Beyoncé was blasting from the stereo in the kitchen. The cook was singing along with great expressiveness. By the dish pit was a floor-to-ceiling rack, jammed full. And there was more—on the floor and on every surface available were dirty pots, pans, and mixing bowls from the night cooks.

There were three large sinks—wash, rinse, sanitize—and a giant sanitizing machine. Gene turned on the sinks to fill them, put on gloves, then went to work. He cleared about half the dish pit, then got stuck for several minutes on a speck of egg on a large stainless pan. He scrubbed and scrubbed furiously, then pulled it from the water to look.

Under the bright lights of the dish pit, the soaps suds slowly spread, revealing the bright yellow bit of egg, still there.

"Fuck this pan!" he shouted.

The cook working at the stoves near the dish pit repeated Gene's frustrated sentiment, smiling in solidarity. She then went to the stove and slid a giant cast iron pan around violently, causing flames to rise to the ceiling.

The cook was twenty-six years old and had worked such jobs since age sixteen. She also cleaned houses on the side. She gave Gene advice six months prior—when he first started the laborious job and his body would shut down during ten-minute breaks, when it was nearly impossible to do anything after work but lay down.

She said, simply, "You can't give them everything; you just have to keep going."

The cake decorator rolled a giant, stainless mixing bowl from the bakery department to the entrance of the dish pit, saying thank you from behind her facemask. She was a single mother who also worked at Whole Foods full time. She wore bell bottom jeans to work every day, spinning cakes around on small turntables while putting icing on them.

Gene went to pick up the mixing bowl, making sure to bend his knees as he did. It had remnants of chocolate frosting inside. He put the stainless egg pan through the sanitizer machine, finally, and went to work on the mixing bowl.

After about an hour, the dish pit was cleared. It was time to pull the chickens from the rotisserie. He grabbed the cart again, a large plastic tray, a set of tongs, gloves for the oven, twelve green plastic bags for the organic chickens, and twelve white plastic bags for the normal chickens. When he opened the rotisserie, a cloud of chicken steam overcame him, filling the store with the smell of hot, greasy chicken.

As customers waited nearby anxiously, he packed them into the bags, using metal tongs to pick up the hot chickens by the cloaca. He zipped each one, printed labels from the cash register to go on the bags of chickens, then rolled them on the cart through the doors of the service counter, putting them on the hot shelf for eager customers to take.

There were many people in the store. They seemed like they were all on vacation, not shopping but more perusing. Many wore exercise clothes, apparently just having come from yoga class. Gene envied how clean and dry they looked, taking a great deal of time to read the nutrition labels on various food items, concerned greatly about their "wellness," "mindfulness," and "spirituality," holding coffees or bottles of kombucha, living in the "experience" economy.

He finished putting the chickens on display and went back through the swinging doors. The dish rack was jammed full again. He left it for later and went out to smoke.

He sat out on the curb and lit a cigarette. He felt dishwashing water squishing in his boots as he took a drag. He had bought commercial fishing gear, in the hopes of alleviating the trench foot he suffered, but it didn't work. He looked at the burning ember on the end of his cigarette, and his fingernails, black and blue and some lifting from getting smashed between heavy pots and pans. Across the narrow roadway in the parking garage was a large dumpster by the loading dock for Ross Dress for Less. It was covered with many black and white shipping labels that the delivery driver stuck on after each delivery. Finches were flying about in the garage, singing cheerfully under the concrete rafters. The Moon shone in the blue sky through a crack between the concrete buildings.

"Walden Pond, indeed," Gene thought, putting out the cigarette and getting up to go face the mountain of dishes waiting inside.

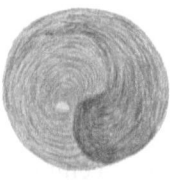

CHAPTER 17

The Reprieve

After a few nights in the freezing streets, Gene moved to an Airbnb in an old boarding house by DuPont Circle. DuPont Circle was a giant roundabout several blocks northwest of the White House, with a grassy park and statue in the middle.

He awoke the morning of November 7, 2020. There were sounds of cheering in the streets outside. Car horns were honking. He went to the window—it looked like World War II had just ended. The roundabout of DuPont Circle was jammed with cars and people. He turned on the television. Joe Biden had been announced the winner of the U.S. presidential election.

Gene headed out into the jubilant streets, carrying his sign with him. Out in the streets, there was a feeling that America had returned to "normal."

Finally, it once again had a Baby Boomer (more or less) at the helm who wore a shit-eating grin and said nice, bread-and-butter things, as establishment politicians do. He would paternalistically guide the country back to its good old-fashioned roots of baseball games and Scranton ice cream parlors, things he took for granted as an heir of the post-WWII American strength and solidarity, funding the purported "Green New Deal" while approving the Willow Project, which would put the final nail into the coffin of human civilization.

Gene walked through BLM plaza, which was packed with young people celebrating and climbing up light posts to shotgun beers for cameras below. He continued to the southern entrance of the White House, where he held up his sign for the Republican Senators who, as Lindsey Graham had announced days before, were going to meet White House officials to get "the story" they were to tell about the election. Just as announced, they came winding down in a line of black SUVs from Capitol Hill, turning into the entrance of the White House, ignoring Gene's sign through dark tinted windows.

A week later, liberals who had filled the streets in celebration of Biden's win were settling into a four-year reprieve—back to their jobs, or back to yoga class to work on "wellness," mindfulness," and "spirituality." Gene was still there, now in front of the Supreme Court, holding his sign. There was a couple taking wedding day photos on the steps of the Court, apparently married by one of the Justices inside. At the top of the giant marble steps, the silhouette of the lonesome guard was still quietly pacing back and forth, in front of the huge wooden doors to the Court that was locked with heavy padlocks.

Then a van arrived, and many people poured out. They looked very different from people he had seen in the weeks prior around D.C. They were mostly white, and all bedecked in bright clothing of red, white, and blue. They pulled signs from the back of the van, also of red, white, and blue. The van then drove away.

The people joined Gene, lingering by the steps of the Supreme Court. They held their signs, and Gene held his. A large, buxom woman from the Midwest moved a bit closer to Gene, looking up at his cardboard sign mounted on wooden sticks.

"What is that?" she asked with a questioning look.

Gene gave a brief explanation. She took no issue with it, but immediately contradicted the message, somewhat, with an explanation about a "loophole" in the U.S. Constitution that could be used to take election decisions away from voters. Gene did not point out that such a loophole could ultimately leave Americans with no recourse, if and when they later wanted a real democracy.

There was no reason to argue. They were on the same side, and it was nice to have some friendly company after weeks in the empty, windswept spaces of D.C. in November 2020.

By the next day, thousands more like those in the van arrived in D.C. They marched down Pennsylvania Avenue, from the White House toward Capitol Hill, waving signs that said:

"STOP THE STEAL"
"MAKE LIBERALS CRY AGAIN!"
"FUCK YOUR FEELINGS!"

The white rotunda of the Capitol building loomed in the distance at the end of the broad boulevard where they were headed. Gene sat against a wall, watching them pass by, letting his eyes relax until the red and blue became blurs of purple, thinking about the supposed divisions in the country.

John Steinbeck likely would identify himself as "conservative," were he still alive. His writings, especially later in his life, excoriated the degeneration of Americans from the Greatest Generation that he knew—those who endured the Great Depression, who fought World Wars, who defeated Fascism, who knew more of the carburetor of the Model T than the clitoris—to whining babies.

He would probably have looked askance at the stereotypical "liberals" who stand by like Thoreau, spouting their untested opinions, demanding rights from a porch of a cabin built on someone else's land, pointing their fingers at the fools who break the ice in winter so the train can run on its tracks, sipping coffee in a comfortable environment of delusion. By the same token, Steinbeck would probably have harsh words for those stereotypical "conservatives" of today, who—also believing comfortable lies— stand ready to cede democracy out of spite, or for lack of a better way to act upon their frustrations. Being an American, he would have sought to reconcile divided thinking, combining the Romantic and the Rational to create the Ideal. His epic novel, *East of Eden*,[16] is good evidence.

The book is set in the Salinas Valley of California, at the end of the Great Depression and beginning of World War II. His character, "Lee," is a Chinese American who acts as a servant for the Trask family, a servant who offers wise advice to his master. Lee spends his free time with a group of old Chinese men who engage in philosophical conversations, while smoking a bit of opium.[17]

---

[16] John Steinbeck, *East of Eden*, Penguin Books (Viking Press, 1952), https://hitalki.org/blog/wp-content/uploads/2023/05/East-of-Eden.pdf.

[17] *See id.* at p. 350.

The philosophers become focused on the story of Cain and Abel in the book of Genesis. Cain and Abel are the sons of Adam and Eve, the first generation of mankind. Divisions appear from the beginning—not unlike those divisions of today in America.

Abel is, on the one hand, the nurturing Romantic—a tender and loving caregiver to helpless, living things. Cain, on the other hand, is the Tiller of the Ground, using Rationalism, Pragmatism, and Common Sense to "subdue" the Earth.[18]

Abel offers to God the "firstlings of his flock and the fat thereof," and God is pleased.[19] Cain, on the other hand, offers "the fruit of the ground" that he tills.[20]

Strangely, God rejects Cain's offering. Why?

Cain becomes jealous of his brother and resentful at God, at which point God asks him—mysteriously—several hard, rhetorical questions, seeming to present a challenge to overcome this anger and reflect on his motives:

---

[18] *See* Genesis 4:2 (KJV) ("And Abel was a keeper of sheep, but Cain was a tiller of the ground.").

[19] Genesis 4:4 (KJV) ("And Abel, he also brought of the first-lings of his flock and of the fat thereof. And the Lord had respect unto Abel and to his offering.").

[20] *Id.* at 4:3.

> "Why art thou wroth? and why is
> thy countenance fallen? If thou doest
> well, shalt thou not be accepted? and
> if thou doest not well, sin lieth at the
> door. And unto thee shall be his desire,
> and thou shalt rule over him."[21]

Lee and his old, opium-smoking philosophers friends contemplate this admonition, wondering if it is a command—that Cain "shalt" rule over sin—or a choice?

After consulting with the Chinese sages in San Francisco, Lee has a revelation, based on the meaning of the word "timshel"—in the Hebrew version. He explains the impact of the word—on the question of man's free will—ecstatically:

> "Don't you see?" he cried. "The American
> Standard translation orders men to
> triumph over sin, and you can call sin
> ignorance. The King James translation
> makes a promise in 'Thou shalt,' meaning
> that men will surely triumph over sin.
> But the Hebrew word, the word *timshel*—
> 'Thou mayest'—that gives a choice."[22]

---

[21] Genesis 4:6-7 (KJV).
[22] Steinbeck, *East of Eden, supra*, at p. 351-52.

A gang of men in bulletproof vests and tactical gear jumped over a retainer wall by the National Archives onto Pennsylvania Avenue, following the parade that has just passed. Most of the men were white, with shaved heads and goatees. The way they moved evidenced a readiness to fight, their presence reminding Gene of Belfast, Northern Ireland, long ago. They were Proud Boys, come to D.C. for the election. They looked prepared to kill their other half, like Cain picking up a stone to strike his own romantic, dreamy brother, bringing hate and division to the Garden of Eden in service to the Devil, bound to live in the Land of Nod. But their Canadian founder, the "godfather of hipsterism," was off somewhere else, laughing at his ironic joke.[23]

Gene attached the sign he had carried for weeks to the high black fence in BLM plaza, making sure not to block other signs. He then walked a bit up

---

[23] *See* Christopher Mathias, "The Proud Boys, The GOP And 'The Fascist Creep'", Huff Post, Oct. 17, 2018 (updated Oct. 18, 2018), https://www.huffpost.com/entry/proud-boys-republican-party-fascist-creep_n_5bc7b-37de4b055bc947d2a8c ("Gavin McInnes, the founder of the violent neo-fascist gang the Proud Boys. . . ."); *see also* WNBC, "'Vice' Founder Gavin McInnes on Split From Glossy: 'It's Like a Divorce,'" Apr. 21, 2010 (© 2024, NBCUniversal Media, LLC), https://www.nbcnewyork.com/local/gavin-mcinnes-on-vice-i-havent-seen-it-in-a-while/1911068/ ("*Vice* magazine's Gavin McInnes, godfather of hipsterdom. . . .").

16th Street and turned around to look once more. The news cameras were gone. The street the next block up was open again. Cars rushed past at the busy intersection. The 2020 Election was over. It was a normal day in America.

The road where he stood was painted with giant yellow letters, proclaiming:

BLACK LIVES MATTER

The old men were still sitting up against the high black fence, with gray beards and black berets, gazing out at scattered clusters of young people in the plaza. Behind them, the White House gleamed in the distance, lit by spotlights. Scaffolding surrounded the buildings for construction repairs. In the foreground was a cardboard sign, duct-taped to wooden sticks and freshly zip-tied to the high black fence, saying:

GOP SENATORS:
NO BELARUS AUTHORITARIANISM
IN THE UNITED STATES
OF AMERICA

Gene's plane took off over the lights of monuments, government buildings, and sterilized office campuses of thousands of businesses capitalizing on D.C. power, then turned west. Gene pressed his face against the cold window of the airplane, looking out at America.

In the sky high above were Cassiopeia and the Big Dipper, those giant and noble constellations circling the North Star like two hands on a clock. Below was a continent that curved around the Earth for three thousand miles, from the Atlantic Ocean to the Pacific. The stars twinkled brightly in the cold, still air of late November.

At intervals, shining cosmic clouds of great cities floated past in the expansive darkness. In between were highways and byways and the small firelight of towns and villages where Americans huddled against the cold of late November, sending silvery lines rising from over the horizon, lit by an orange glow below.

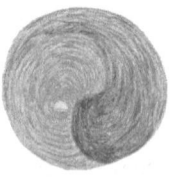

CHAPTER 18

The Masses

There was something on the ground. The wanderer stopped. He knelt and looked at it closely. There was a picture of a man. There were also horrendous shapes—words—in contrast to the grassland and sky and all natural forms he had known. The words said:

DRIVER'S LICENSE
DISTRICT OF COLUMBIA
DC0034891
SMITH, EUGENE

Then the air filled with the sound of voices and people moving through the grass toward him. It was a great mass of others, like him, all walking in the same direction. He stood, unconsciously picking up the card on the ground as he did.

Someone bumped into him, then another. He was pushed and shoved. Soon, he was also walking in the masses, going to see where they were headed, holding the thing he had found on the ground.

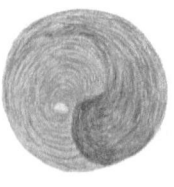

CHAPTER 19

The Coast

Fog floated low in scattered patches over the grassland. The air grew cooler. He came to a cliff above the sea and looked down. The waves crashed against the rocky shoreline below, sounding like roaring lions in the night. The Moon shone upon the sea.

He felt the presence of another. A little way off, the silhouette of a man stood, staring up at the Moon. His lips were moving, speaking without sound. It was the old warrior he had encountered before, with fearsome tattoos.

The warrior noticed the wanderer, slowly turning his head from the Moon to him. They fixed their eyes for a moment. The old warrior then nodded, finally returning his gaze back to the Moon. The wanderer stood watching as the warrior's lips began to move again in silent conversation. He then climbed down to the water below.

A gentle breeze blew on his wet skin. He floated on the water, watching the stars falling, one by one, into the black horizon of sky and sea. On the horizon there were lights—two white, one over the other, and a green light below, moving slowly up the coast, then disappearing around a point of land.

A wall of blackness was moving toward him now, blocking out the stars. He turned toward the shore and paddled, looking over his shoulder, trying to make out the contours of the approaching form in the darkness. It began to lift and push him. He paddled harder, then finally stood.

He slid down the face of the wave, putting pressure on his toes, easing into a slow turn at the bottom. His fingertips skimmed the wall of water standing vertically by his side. The top of the wave was outlined by a white line of spray from the offshore breeze against the black sky, lit by the Moon, forming rainbows in silver tones above.

The wall of water beside him teetered, began to bend, then flew over his head and down like a guillotine on the other side of him. A ball of foam exploded under his feet. He used all the power of his legs to steady himself.

The curtain of the falling wave fell further and further ahead, like a raging river encircling him, pulling him deeper and deeper inside a spinning cavern of encapsulated air.

He took a breath, holding it in, and placed his hands on his chest. Inside, there was a strange, rhythmic beating.

He held the breath in, looking up at the Moon, dancing through the watery ceiling, lighting the tunnel with hues of purple and green—until swallowed by the merciless sea.

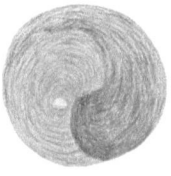

CHAPTER 20

The One

A warm blanket of air blew over him as he slept. The Big Dipper was rising. Cassiopeia and Orion blazed high above. Jupiter fell in the west. The tall grass around him rustled in the wind. Crickets chirped. Coyotes howled in the distance. An owl flew over, made a great turn, then passed over once again to get a second look at the human asleep on the open grassland.

Silky hair brushed against his skin. Then a gentle hand rested on his shoulder. He awoke and opened his eyes.

Her eyes sparkled with the light of the Moon, looking down at him.

She smiled, then whispered, "Come back to the fire."

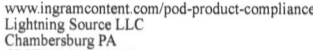